Music From Behind a Stone Wall

Text set in Century Gothic & Garamond 3 LT Std

Cover, layout & design by Sharon Zetter
Cover image: Orpheus playing the vihuela: frontispiece to Luis de Milán's
book of vihuela music, El Maestro (1536)

Printed in the United States
by Books International, Dulles, Virginia
Acid Free Archival Quality Recycled Paper

Library of Congress Cataloging-in-Publication Data

Names: Rood, Steven, 1949- author.
Title: Music from behind a stone wall : poems / Steven Rood.
Description: Oakland : Omnidawn Publishing, 2024. | Summary: "Poems as
music arise from the poet's sixty years as a classical guitarist and his
preoccupation with the tonalities of day-to-day life. Each poem in the
book contributes to a multi-orchestrated symphony encompassing the
delights and travails of family life and the moments of intimate
connection with the animals and plants with which the poet comes into
contact. At the core of the book are poems delving into the nearly
impossible task to communicate the essence of a musical experience using
the written word. It is a book of grief and joy sung with lyric acuity,
imagistic surprise, and formal variation"-- Provided by publisher.
Identifiers: LCCN 2024002644 | ISBN 9781632431271 (trade paperback)
Subjects: BISAC: POETRY / American / General | POETRY / Subjects & Themes /
Death, Grief, Loss | LCGFT: Poetry.
Classification: LCC PS3618.O666 M87 2024 | DDC 811/.6--dc23/eng/20240118
LC record available at https://lccn.loc.gov/2024002644

Published by Omnidawn Publishing, Oakland, California
www.omnidawn.com   (510) 237-5472   (800) 792-4957
10 9 8 7 6 5 4 3 2 1
ISBN: 978-1-63243-127-1

MUSIC

FROM

BEHIND

A

STONE

WALL

STEVEN ROOD

OMNIDAWN PUBLISHING
OAKLAND, CALIFORNIA
2024

Also by STEVEN ROOD:

Naming the Wind, Omnidawn Publishing (2022)

CONTENTS

To Marcia Falk: life-partner,
poetry-partner, parent-partner.

To Abraham Falk-Rood: mi hijo,
mi compañero.

MEMOIR

My first teachers were a street lamp at dusk,
the smell of dry sycamore leaves,
and the supper-bell.
From them I learned loneliness,
precursor to music.
Then came rain. Mist-like,
followed by drops, short and round,
teaching distinction within noise.
Then came sunlight dissolving clouds,
teaching transparency.
Then night sky, where I learned silence
between notes.
Wind taught momentum,
dreams dissonance.
From language came the phrase.
From moving leaves came touch.
My last teacher was age.
It taught me to remember.

PSYCHOANALYSIS

My psyche is a meadow of stones,
surrounded by stone walls rattling with crickets
and covered with starry and staghorn mosses, lichens, ferns, liverworts.
Walls sheltering voles and garter snakes.
My libido is warm stones hidden under clover and dung.
My unconscious is plow-broken stones, covered by hay.
Every spring new stones rise up from under the stone-ridden farm.
I've dug and piled for decades.
The walls are impermanent—
disintegrating, restless, knocked over by cows.
I've also built a cairn of stones—twelve-foot high cylinder
hidden in stands of the relentless maples.
A dark column, fitted and trimmed.
The cairn abides.

UNTIL AMNON ARRIVED

At thirteen, I'd had only Cantor Michelson chanting Torah,
and, on my parents' radio, Peggy Lee and Frank Sinatra.
After school, I'd go next door to listen to Amnon hold forth.
One day he asked: "Stevie, do you want to hear something
    on the phonograph?"
Before I answered, the arm swung,
descended, scratched into the grooves.
The New York Pro Musica's madrigals of Claudio Monteverdi.
I lay on the floor next to the couch. *Ecco mormorar l'onde.*
Four voices like watersnakes entwining in a creek pool
    overhung with lilies.
Kingfishers, hoopoes, quail, morning light in Italy.
The small houses of my suburb vibrating like lutes.

TO EXCAPE

my house, filled with chattering neighbors,
I'd walk along Sunset Terrace toward the nearby hill.
I did not have the words for what happened,
and for what, at ten years old, I already was.
Fifty years later I could say "odd-boy-who-was-not-seen."
I left the noise and found things that couldn't talk back.
Tree. Bush. Skipper moth. Wind.
I found rock. Underlying my whole neighborhood
were fine siltstone layers (I later learned),
between which were pressed tiny crystallized fish,
laid down in the warm inland seas of the Holocene.

ATTRIBUTES OF MUSIC

God did not create music.
His creatures David, Orpheus, and Sappho did.
Music commands nothing.
Is composed of forces
that entangle ears, neurons, mystery.
Sound stained by memory is music.
What Gesualdo wrote three centuries ago,
shatters glass in my hands.
It is the shatter I want.

NONETHELESS

Literalism kills the spectral inside the between.
I worry that my love of what wind does to the sycamores at dusk
marks me a Romantic. Can I still be that innocent at seventy-five?
I walk amid real things of the forest, attempting to see their reality.
I encounter the same Muscovy duck every day for two months:
blistered face, malachite-green-indigo-black body feathers, white wings.
I have the leisure to wait until squirrels are willing to sit on my lap.
I watch mushrooms push their wet spears through the duff overnight.
The flying goose brings the message: it is good to remain here, on earth.

CONVERSATION

If you insist on asking me how I am,
I could say nothing. Which is honest enough.
Most honest is the music. A clear sea.
On its skin, if I play the guitar strings as waves,
the various weathers will erupt.
At an angle, the eye penetrates
to where black fish move
in smooth procession, and below them,
the blocks and columns of my ruined acropolis.

HELPLESS

Responsibility is lenient this afternoon
and does not overwhelm the subtle healing
of sun and shade, rock and water.
There's no one else in the park,
except for the boy who dwells in my chest,
intact and perfect.
Occasionally he reminds me he's still here.
I feel him feel the extinctions of geese and ducks.
The boy is puzzled by all of it,
and I can't help either of us.
There is only the scrape of birds' feet
in the leaf-litter, and we listen together.

THE KEYS

C Major: The music started when I was three,
playing amid camellias and dirt;
sunlit lawns and my mother's hand rhythmically patting my back.
G major: the first sharp, five years old, when Cathy kicked my shins.
D major, at ten, my first folk song:
"The fox went out on a chilly night,
and prayed for the moon to give him light."
A major, three sharps: the little dance I did
when Cathy touched my thigh at thirteen.
E major, four sharps: both a bright Bach partita
and the blues I played on the stoop of my freshman apartment.
F-sharp major, and my life was swarming with sharps:
first marriage at twenty-five, first job as a lawyer defending the rich.
Then came the relative minor keys.
A minor with shadows along the mossy brick wall at dusk.
E minor: Selma Teretsky's death by cancer when I was thirty-five;
she who insisted that writing legal briefs was crippling my hands.
I still did not believe death applied to me.
B minor, two sharps: the first big failures: marriage, job.
Then the decade of flats: when I sat drunk every night in front of the TV.
F-sharp major returned with all those sharps, when I was sixty.
I know death now: parents, friends, mentors, relatives.
From there, it is only a half-step back to C Major.
I play slowly, according to the diminished dexterity of my hands.
There is an animal, maybe a wolf,
calling to me from outside the stone wall.

EMPATHY

Skin as portal, not as cover.
You run your fingernail along my wrist,
which opens to the quick-land
where we meet each other.
Sparrows nest under my nipples.
It's painful when each chick opens its eyes.

RUIN

Cocteau was asked what he would save
if his house were burning. "The fire."
If my house were burning,
I would save my guitar even as the fire singed its body.
I would smell the particular woods it was made of,
there in Granada in 1962. Rosewood, ebony, spruce.
I'd feel how the thin threads of nerves burn in my hands
when I play the fantasias of Milán, the fugues of Bach.
If the guitar had burned, I would still feel
its warmth remaining as a stamp in the soft metal of my chest.
I would keep the ruin of it near my desk,
so I could smell the residue of its shape
as I typed how I would have burned with it.

MARCH 1963: FIRST KISS

One solar system, Trappist-1, collides with another, Kepler 16b.
These universes are almost unknown to themselves,
let alone to the other.
There are trillions of solar systems in the cosmos.
No one can explain the liquefied mystery that happens when they meet.
Often a system holds out its hand,
but it passes through the other, unnoticed.
To be honest is to be confused.
So much willful forgetting of the tiny, dying animals we are,
creatures who don't have a hint
about what really turns us into liquid, solid, fire, or mist.

UNDER NOISE

I play the lute on gut strings
stretched over a bowl
of pearwood and spruce.
Muscles, sinews, tendons thrum deep into my limbic.
Deeper than limbic to the spine,
to the cord that links the organs of gender
with the lit fuses of brain.
Sometimes I'm stretched so taut I might break.
Other times I play like water flexing over creek-stones.
I'm listening to sounds before words can shape them.
To undertones carried by winds.
To the ground-tone under engines
and crackling circuits.
To the hum of the origin.

CRACKS

Perfection of shape makes no sound.
Air passes over the flawless wing silently.
Smoothness permits no din or tumult.
By virtue of turbulence, wind speaks.
Weeds and trees push through clefts.
The rarest chasmophytes cling
to gorge-walls and crevices:
bellflower, skullcap, samphire, catchfly.
In the flaw, fissure, schism, fracture,
is sweet speech. By split chords,
the human noise. Music.

STEADFAST OAK

The axis runs from my cock to the Evening Star.
From molten red at the center of the earth, to my orange intestines,

yellow plexus, green heart, blue mouth, purple cortex—
then up and out of my crown into the absolute.

The axis runs through nights of Jerusalem and Oakland.

The earth is resonance
that I needn't decipher to feel its frequencies.

My belly is the pond surrounded by cattails
and inhabited by carp, frogs, salamanders, two coots.

My heart is the commons.

My cranium is the Empress Tree.

My mouth is the conclusion and the consequence.
The mouth, which is me speaking from dirt to sun.

I FELT THE VIOLIN INSIDE ME

Faint and almost transparent,
a slender thread that began
to shape. Not recognizable yet
as part of a larger thing.
Not melody or harmony,
but increasingly strong.
Far off, but clear.
Like the violin of the Russian
who lived above Zion Square.
I'd stand on the street, listening
to music from behind the stone walls.
Suddenly a thousand notes
were cascading mayflies
above the steaming spring mud.

WHO SENT THIS HAWK?

Not the rabbis or my parents,
but a night wind from across the membrane of death.
The hawk lights on my head, spreads its wings
over my shoulders. Will its talons pierce my scalp?
Its beak tear my neck? But it settles, as I settle.
After Jack died he became a fox.
Jud a sloth. Melvin a beaver.
Bessie a parakeet. Rose a chicken.
This hawk is no one I know.
I see bands on the flight feathers
and the rust-colored fan of the tail.
I am half this bird already.

THE OAK GROVE ON PIEDMONT WAY
SLATED TO BE CUT DOWN BY THE UNIVERSITY

The grove's only voice is wind,
a chorus of soft lisps.
A tree cannot persuade,
helpless against argument and money.
A tree's effect is music without words.
Spreading out from a still center.
Then blooming into time,
shapes, exultation, grief,
and the many orders of green.
The only way for a tree to prevail
is for a human to yield to it completely.
The way I might sometimes permit music to enter me.
Perhaps when I'm tired or sick.
Then sound is suspended
until a silence glows around it,
and at once I shake
for holding so much.
Phrases, movements, skies
winds, meadows.
The oaks applying their thousand subtle fingers
to peel me.

CHRISTMAS DAY, NORTH FACE OF MOUNT DIABLO

Inside the dark blue-mauve shadows of Coulter pines.
Then down into the refrigerator of a green-black canyon.
Deeper down into a wet blue-black gorge.
Coyotes briefly high-singing
—at the moment of dusk-turned-night—*We are here.*
Me alone on the mountain,
thousand-meter height and five-kilometer girth.
By flashlight, I illuminate liverworts, starry mosses,
licorice ferns, live-forevers
on rock scarps above Back Creek.
Two-thousand years since Jesus: an afternoon nap.

KIBBUTZ RAMAT RACHEL

This afternoon—amid pine, oak, hawthorn, lentisk, terebinth—
I'm walking alone in the archaeological site on the kibbutz grounds.
A few hundred meters away, I can see the crowds swimming in the rec pool.
Between toppled blocks of the King of Judah's palace
arise alkanet, bugloss, heliotrope, lotus, mallow, squill, asphodel.
A kilometer away, beyond groves of olive trees, is an Arab village
where men put down prayer rugs on crushed limestone.
I walk near burial caves and pits that were ritual baths.
A score of civilizations have come and gone.
At the edge of the ruins, Zionists cut defensive trenches.
I can feel the crunch of pottery shards and flint chips through my shoes.

TODAY I LEARNED

that the green covered public trash bins open with a foot pedal;
that what I thought was a hummingbird is a Sunbird,
the national bird of Palestine. It had rested for seconds
on the pepper tree, then flitted away. He's known as "the flying gem."
In a month or so, I might learn enough to ask for pizza with olives
in Hebrew and not be stared at. I am recognized here as not a danger,
my face apparently Jewish enough, though I see soldiers looking hard.
I try to make contact with cats and to learn types of birds and plants.
I feel at home among them, because they are not political
and have universal names that do not depend on local languages:
Pistacia palaestina, Nectarinia osea, Felis catus.
The human communities are more complicated.
Though I smile at everybody, only some children smile back.

LUIS DE NARVÁEZ, *FANTASIA XIV* FOR VIHUELA

The spring drips clear ichor onto the travertine cliff
and falls into descending creek pools.
Three kinds of ferns tremble in the small winds
released by the falling waters:
bird's foot, licorice, maidenhair.
The last pool is the deepest lens into my mind.
When I play the vihuela, a Spanish Renaissance proto-guitar,
my right hand plucks, my left palpates the fingerboard—
forming the changing shapes that become music, which is the spring
spilling its clear ichor from mind to mind to hands.

THE WORLD TO COME

This wind was born in the Atlantic, crossed the Great Sea,
rushed up the Judean hills. Scented by hot limestone and mastic,
this wind pushed into the Hinnom burial caves, merged with dust,
then reached my apartment's garden. I am a still point amid ignited trees.
Wind is young. Ruins are old. A millimeter beneath the Bronze Age
is rock older than all human rage. I want to remain in this world,
where I work and rest. Wind confuses time. My path is unclear.

THE BOY SAYS YES, THE BOY SAYS NO

This little boy goes to market
to pick up corn and a brisket for Mommy.
This little boy runs home.
Why does he feel hot-necked in the store?
Why does he lock the bathroom door?
Why stuff bread in his mouth
while Daddy—who doesn't make enough
selling used batteries—slams the table?
Up Sunshine Terrace this boy goes,
to the wild hill behind the house.
He finds sugary, spiky veins of quartz
laminated in slabs of siltstone
and laced with fossils of fish and ferns.
This boy brings a crystal home,
buries it in loam under the camellias,
then forgets for a decade.
Finds it again in high school.
Quartz, the young man learns,
is 7 on the Mohs hardness scale.
Common. Clear with flaws. Lasts for eons.

WALK: 12/12/22

At dusk, I watch a family through their big front window.
Girls, mother, grandmother setting a table
and bringing in a plate of brisket and roasted potatoes.
The youngest sees me see her. I am the first to turn away.
On my way uphill, I take two apricots
from a tree near the sidewalk,
and three tough, seedy tangerines.
I reach a park, where one boy skateboards.
His mind is an alien solar system
in which little furious planets and moons spin.
I am a faraway, dense, cold star, almost invisible.
I remember how my son and I would go around town
looking for fruit trees to raid.
And how, when he was a baby,
I would take him out in his stroller.
How he'd quiet in the shaking dusk.
We'd look right through houses into the turquoise sky
and the sun setting through orange silks of the tails of fish.

FINDING MY CALLING AT FIFTEEN
IN AN ABANDONED MINE

Rock-roof met floor-pool in the last available light.
It was either swim underwater toward god-knows-where
or go back. I went on.
Big breath and five strokes into blackness.
Crawled out on a mud bank. Thought of newts.
Didn't remember bringing matches,
but dug through my pockets to find them dry in a match-safe.
Struck one. There was air. Discovered a dome-room.
Looked for shining ores. Only dull, soft sandstone.
Wondered why this tunnel had been dug at all. For gold? Coal?
Or nothing but somebody's idea to enter a mountain?
To get away from the jumbled conglomerates of the outer world?
I stayed in the room through six matches-worth of time,
having no thought that my whole life could have been snuffed out there.
Swam again, then crouched along toward the glinting coin of light.

GEODES

We look for lumpy egg-shapes, weighing their uncanny lightness,
which might mean they're hollow with ingrown crystals.
A tractor scrapes across the high desert scrub.
Is it a mile away, or ten?
"I love this heat," I say to my son at the Acton Country Store,
where we've come to save ourselves with icy Cokes.
The man who overhears says, "It's good to know what you love."
Yes, I think. Worn-away places. Worn people who abide, nonetheless.
The rough skins of rocks that crack off to show milky agates inside.
Abandoned gravel pits. A bleached creosote bush.
Stones that outlast soft things. Soft things in their flourishing.
Sky-blue flower-cups rising out of cracked chert.
The rabbit bounding through hot basalt beds.
The furnace of noon crushing my face.
Looking down at wastes and up into vastness.
So the middle can be exceptionally clear.

WAYS OF KNOWING

I don't remember most of the Thirteen Principles of Faith,
authored by the Spanish medieval Jew, Maimonides,
though I chanted his words every Saturday in shul.
I do remember that the dead will be raised—the thirteenth principle.
I don't remember all the Latin names of ferns.
I do recognize the way the one with round fingers
moves with the small winds rising from the creek.
The rabbis of the Talmud didn't care to remember the names of trees.
"It's a kind of tree," they would say.
I know trees the way the rabbis did, by function.
What kind of fruit: tasty or sickening?
Does the tree mark the edge of a backyard or a cemetery?
Is it lumber or does it yield a sweet sap?
Is it the kind of tree where mushrooms I like to eat
grow between its knuckles and legs?
Or the kind that makes me remember it
because it is burning and I am inside?

GRANADA, 1962

The guitar-maker stored the wood for the guitar's body in a shed
where it seasoned in heat. Spiders and rats nested there.
The wood dried so purely it rang at the scrape of his nails.
It became resonant as metal,
sensitive as the face of a pond to night wind.
The man who steamed it into shape smoked filthy cigars,
boiled his glues from horses he slaughtered,
brewed stains from crushed walnuts,
and spat tobacco juice into his lacquer. He refused varnish
and the fine tuning heads that modern custom demanded.
His fingers were too thick to play the guitars he made.
When I got the thing, no one wanted to touch it.
Give it to the boy, he needs a beginner's guitar.
The perfume, the rosette, the ebony, the frets—
a civilization. At thirteen, I became a citizen
of its unreasonable and Moorish beauty, harvesting
for decades what it would make of me.
Even when my own fingers thickened,
and I couldn't play much,
I could smell the forest inside.

I KNOW MYSELF

by the glowing ochre slot canyon hung with polypody ferns;

by a pot of stewed prunes and carrots; frying onions;

by a recording of Monteverdi madrigals by the New York Pro Musica,
which I heard by accident when I was thirteen.

I discovered that sound alone could magnetize a whole boy.

Now, it is how to hold on gently to disappearance.

SHRINKING

This year melts into a dun-colored November.
Five deer, mothers and fauns, move in line across the wet field.
The orange spectacle of October is gone.
Jews listen to their candles gutter, which makes a melancholy they prize.
Evergreens persist amid the bare hardwoods.
When was the world not always ending?
If family strife, if disease, if war, if catastrophe, if death?
I feel my body's change toward dusk.
What's left? Mice I share the kitchen with.
My family. Those few friends who didn't leave me for cause.
Let me buy you some ice cream, and we can talk until we say, "Enough."

IMMORTAL TECHNIQUE

Time and pitch, sharp in my throat, yield a voice.
Music forms the conjunction of wind and leaves,
in the distance between perishing and an iris.
The hairs in its flower-throat
are fine gold, with the powder of generation in them.
The hairs in my throat scale toward music.
I started as a brio-tenor, ended as a root-bass.

THE GREAT WORK

Wind, leaves, sunlight, wet-mind
alchemize in the space between them.
I sit, indolent, under sixty feet of sycamore—
citrine, orange, red, brown.
The tree gives rattle to the wind.
Sheds scraps of its crown to the soil.
Provides limbs for crows settle in at night,
where they light up the tree into consciousness.
Sends roots into an underworld
electrified by fungal nets.
Under this tree's aegis,
I'm neither angry nor scattered.
My eyes detonate rainbows.

WALK: 6/20/23

Why would I want to get drunk,
if, in the fourteen billion years of this cosmos,
I have only this time to experience it?
Why would I want to numb up and watch TV,
if, in June only of each year, a particular
lily, *Calochortus tiburonensis*, blooms
inconspicuously on one mountain—
made of hot serpentine rock—
that I hike hard to get to?
Why would I voluntarily give up
witnessing its nectaries glisten
under fine hairs in the flower's throat?

MONTARA BEACH

Winter sea on my right, bald coastal mountains on my left.
Past white llamas, a stinky paddock.
My legs heavy at first, aching;
then shifting to a smooth, painless stride.
A body forgiving its age. Age forgiving its body.

I remember last month, before I closed my office for good,
I was alone in the stairwell with my guitar, late,
and rather than going home,
I revived a piece I hadn't played for years.
Prelude, Fugue, and Allegro in D Major by J.S. Bach.
It came easily, by dint of the music that had nested whole,
intact, ready in my fingers.

I'm running now,
fluently moving from my regular body to the alternate body inside me.
Running-music, sex-music, music-music—
held and released again into the alternate earth and sea.

NOT IN MAGAZINES

On the street, in the subway,
the office, the next booth,
in the Diane Arbus photographs
of nudists and transvestites.
Most of us flawed, skin unbeautiful,
porky, unkempt, unfortunately hair-doed.
Tired from work of all kinds,
getting older and more bewildered.
Shrinking.
Looking similarly ridiculous, whether
heroes, freaks, partiers, or poets.
Slipping more and more into alcohol,
TV, sleep aids, unfathomable sadness.
Puzzled as the accidents keep happening
over and over, so they begin to resemble fate.
Maybe there really is fate.
That which we are to become, no matter what.
Remember how unaccountable my way was
to the Catskills, where I breathed
for a week, vanishing
amid maples and cows?
Yes, here I am, glistening in the silver portraits,
looking straight into the green eye of God.

PARENTS

The baby latching onto his mother's breast for two years.
Me wiping the baby's nates, inspecting him a dozen times a day.
Holding his foot every night so he'll feel my touch
and be able to calm himself to sleep in his crib-jail.
Then his beginning to feed on solids: first startled lick of pear
on my wife's index fingertip.
Reading bedtime books, the same ones for years.
Singing "Hush little baby," over and over, until he is ten.
Picking up and dropping off. Pointing out birds and snails.
Playing with twigs, pebbles, water.
The endless, exquisite boredom of infinite care.

MISSA IN TEMPORE BELLI
(MASS IN TIME OF WAR)
Franz Joseph Haydn

Our boy's green eyes close. He asks his mother to read
his favorite bedtime book, *Five Minutes Peace*,
about an elephant mother and her three calves.
She reads it every night. Slowly.

The Mass says, *O Lamb of God, Agnus dei*.
But I don't want the *Lamb*. Not *Gloria*. Not *Hosanna*.
Maybe only the music:
Haydn's martial trumpets and tympani.

We breathe in the scent
of the breath of our sleeping boy.

But maybe I don't want the music, either.
Just the sounds a person makes
blowing into a hollowed ram's horn
ripped out of the skull—
like the one our little family saw Rabbi Ferris
boil and pull from a stinking pot.

A raw thing blasting everywhere.
As it was three thousand years ago.
As it may not be next winter.

ASHKELON

I've come to visit the archeological site of the Neolithics—
their clay pots, tools chopped out of flint and raw copper,
and the dents their towns left in empty fields of the Levant.
Their adzes, knives, flesh scrapers, ash pits.
They must have been filled with immensity
as night skies entered them, as spring flowers drenched
their bare feet, as their bodies coupled and danced.
Must have stretched catgut strings over tortoise shells
and found a quiet transport from the outer winds to the interior winds.
Must have swum in the sea and cooked meat and fish
under poplars and palms. They disappeared.
At Ashkelon archeologists are excavating an important village.
The Neolithics seemed to have buried dogs with themselves
in a graveyard next to the shack where I'm served a cold drink.
Everybody wants to cook meat on the beach,
while their babies play with buckets and sand.

LETTER TO A YOUNG FRIEND

You don't need to hear about my operation,
unless it will help you to feel lucky that you are still seventeen.
When I die, you might say a few words to my son,
then forget me, going on with your immortal life
of small things. I am of the generation on the way out.
We look like all other old people since humans began: ugly.
You are beautiful. My son is beautiful.
The world is filled with idiots, frauds, narcissists.
Nothing has been done to cure that.
Ants are Spartans—organized, disciplined, cooperative.
Ants survive. Humans are Athenians—
brilliant, separated, supernal, anarchic.
Humans perish. Your style of thriving will add new luster,
maybe even help to ameliorate the tarnish.
I will tuck this note into the book I'm giving you
for graduation: a new translation of the *Iliad*.

THE POND

No people are here on this 109-degree afternoon.
My companions are geese,
dunking for coolness and bath.
Their long necks hook around themselves
to bill and fluff each part.
Some geese nibble duff in the scant oak-shade.
Goslings imitate the mothers.
All of us quiet. They seem to ignore me
as some of them lay their heads back
into the clefts between folded wings.
I'm relieved to be irrelevant,
unobserved, a shape—
the way the oak trunk is.

THE OTHER VIEW

Wolf spiders wait for anything to touch their webs and stick.
In after-storm sun, the wet webs are galaxies.
A single meadow holds thousands of them.
Man to man is an arrant wolf, wrote Hobbes.
When I was ten, I was a spider-hunter.
I found a black widow in an orange grove
of the San Fernando Valley, when it was a valley of groves.
All spiders are venomous, even if their mouthparts
cannot pierce human skin.
Scientists say the neural codes of spiders are acute and deep.
Deeper even than those of reptiles,
and simpler. As deep as the roots of the wolf trees
of great girth that kill every sapling around them.
As deep as the fine rootlets of the death camas,
their creamy lily-flowers attracting humans.
The roasted bulbs are sweet.

ANNA SIGURDARDOTTIR

How hard you worked, repeating one note, again and again,
for three months, to get the touch right.
Then the phrase for weeks.
I wanted to kill you,
deriding your talent, calling you stupid,
who could sit there,
day after day, playing nothing.
Finally, after I insisted,
you sat before the keys
showering a Partita on me.
Then, convinced, I worked my own hands,
repeating note after note.
And then we discovered
we could sing together, climbing
all over each other, making it up,
making up music beyond touch.

DRIVING

"Fuck you, ass-fuck-bitch!" My cursing even worse now in my seventies
than when I was driving truck in high school for Sierra Tile Company
and unloading 10,000 pounds of grout-bags and ceramic tiles
while being heckled by crews and on-lookers:
"Hey, Jew-boy, haul that fat ass!"
Yet now I'm spewing "Fuck" and "Moron" at mini-van, VW, Tesla.
They can't hear you, my frowning passenger-wife tells me,
but *she* can, and I make her sick with all my bitching.
I like the word "bitch," because it can attach to all sexes, even objects.
Bitch-trucker texting. Bitch-old-man-in-hat going too slow. Bitch-stop-sign.
I will not change my bitching.
My dead grandfathers, father, uncles— all of them bitched
in kitchens at their wives for the over-cooked brisket.
Bitched in their cars at cops, at their sons for being weak.
My rage began at five, when I was ordered to go to law school—
my father's unlived life.
Now my rage is sealed in the air-tight, sound-proof, silver missile.
Our Sages of the Talmud tell us that even God bitches.

WALK: 11/15/22

I walk beside the lawyer in his Armani suit.
People we pass on Broadway say
"Looking good." "Nice suit." "How you doing?"
The young associates laugh at his observations
as they walk with him on the way to afternoon coffee.
Waitresses flirt.
Men glance at his aqua Maserati GranTurismo
with creamy leather seats and burled walnut panels.
I begrudge him none of it.
I have seen shining men quickly pauperized.
Smiles wiped off, houses sold, lawsuits commenced against them.
I have seen what cancer and dementia do.
How people look at a fallen man,
thinking how lucky they are not to be him.
I've been a ruined man.
I remind myself of that every time
I put on the Brioni suit my father had tailored to fit his shrinking body,
and into which I fit almost perfectly.

TWO LIVES

The night breathes into my ear
its starlight. Its leaf- and petal-falls.
Its moon riding the crowns of black firs.
Its baby skunk shuttling along the dirt road.
I'm anxious—despite the vast cosmos around me—
because I will be in trial tomorrow defending a rich man
accused of shoplifting a pair of sunglasses from Ross Dress For Less.
The next morning the man is convicted, banned for life from the store,
and given Community Service. He blames me.
In the neon-lit, bare courtroom, amid the blah-blah,
I hear sparrows in the night-blooming jasmine.

IT IS A COLOR

resembling the darkening evening sky.
The color of the inside
of a black oak at dusk. A canker,
a cramp ball, the color of a crow's breast.
I say it is a lightning-struck pine,
weathered five hundred years,
flesh the color of bitter plum-skin.
The black bearded iris of Anatolia.
The carapace of a stinkbug.
It is Bill Evans on heroin
under blue spotlights and smoke.
It is a spot on Vermeer's sable tip.
The burning blue gas-jets of Cappadocian navelworts
flaring in a field of dry barley.
Larkspur on basalt. Aunt Rose's blue lips.
Veins on the inside of my left wrist.

GUARNERI OF CREMONA

Amid shadows of north slopes,
subjected to wind, freeze, acid soil,
in the Italian Dolomites, only at tree line, grew
the almost starved *Acer pseudoplatanus*,
with chalky, fibrous, powerful wood—
the maple del Gesu prayed for.
His tree was crooked.
He imagined the whole violin
he would carve between its heart and bark.
Knew he'd found an extraordinary blank
the second he touched his chisel lightly to it.
Then worked it obsessively until it was fronds
of uncurling ferns, lids of babies' eyes, a skeleton key.
Finally, so open and clear
it would reveal instantly the nuances of the player.
Highly responsive, therefore dangerous.
Musicians of his day called the violin "monster."
Del Gesu called it a mystery.
Release it.

MINE ALONE

I'd finish a bluebook exam in law school
and file out of the room, along with the other releasees
into wisterias and a sun-blasted courtyard.
The students would talk about this or that
question on hearsay exceptions, choice of law,
unreasonable searches, how they answered them.
A few were smiling, most stricken. I'd get away fast.
My experience of a problem and its solution was mine.
I also run away from rooms with complaining old people.
My inner life is mine. My death is mine.
I keep both of them close, under my vest.
A satchel of meaning hidden there.
A satisfaction that exceeds all the arguments.

THE CONSEQUENCE OF BACH

I play the first note, listen to it carefully
as it rises, swells, then dies in the air of the stairwell.
I linger with it, before the next note finds me.
Two notes together become music.
More become the Allegro and Fugue in D major.
My hands hold the Lüneburg church, its organ,
the organist, stars, winds, heavens.
Sounds become orders of light.
The way a hawk spans herself open
on the clean wind, leaning
into her flight-muscles, adjusting minutely,
to keep hovering for as long as she can.
The music spiraling out of my fingers
in colors, stately and glittering,

MOUNTAIN

I wore new hiking boots, putting on extra-thick "military" socks.
A mistake. Both feet blistered from 3000 feet up, 3000 feet down.
I picked up ticks on both arms. Tried to look cool as I passed other hikers.
On the path, I warned myself about footing—out loud—scouting
danger-spots: "Here is loose gravel on hard clay."
I slid anyway, banging elbows and hands.
When I was sure I wouldn't be seen, I dropped under a hoptree to rest.
Was it the Buddha who said, "Don't look where you don't want to go"?
I wondered if I court falls and pain to inoculate myself against real pain:
failures of kindness, failures to yield to instinct,
failures to enact my dreams.
After sitting for twenty, thirty minutes, my body and mind forgave
me—again—and I limped deeper into the folds of the mountain.
Around me were soap root's spidery flowers suspended
on invisible stem-threads.
I opened a lemony globe lily to touch its intimate, interior hairs.
Looked down at plutonic parasitic ground-cones feeding on chamise-roots.
I squinted and, by mercy, didn't see the part of the mountain
that was eaten away by miners. Listened to the wind
scorching an alder and didn't hear the under-hum of the city.
Reached Donner Creek and splashed my face: I was laved in its brightness.
Then put my ringing feet into a pool overhung with crimson columbines.

FERMATA

The fermata says wait. So, for once, I take it seriously,
holding the rest beyond what is reasonable, and beyond that
into something wild. Staying out there in the wind
as people call for me to get down and play
the next thing. Letting silence increase silence,
until the audience is furious, and I'm shaking with doubt.

But can I deny the rare tingle and ease in my hands,
suspended between furies, when they move like deer,
unforced and fluent up the slope?

Only my son knows how something settles on me
when we're walking, and I stop, and we're quiet.
What if all anyone ever knows of my soul is its shining
interval of silence? What if all they ever have of my music
is the rest? Not words or notes, but the after and before,
coming from the precision of that silence?
What if I stayed with that unborn thing in me?
Entering possibility like it was a cool, limitless sea,
believing anything can happen there under the power of my hands?

MOUNT DIABLO

107 degrees. I'm alone with the smell of what heat does to leaves.
I collapse against a boulder next to Donner Creek,
where burnt-orange ladybugs have massed to cool themselves.
They crawl onto my shoulders.
Furnace-winds, scented with tarweed, empty my cranium of thought.
At last, I pry myself up, begin to wobble, nauseated.
Walking now, feeling my body's limits by slowly exceeding them,
then backing off, staying at the edge of capacity.
I sit again, deliquescing into the earth.
Have I become the moss I once saw in the hollow of an oak?
Is this the kind of death I've wished for?

SWIM

When I was seven, my mother sent me to Cheryl Vitarelli's mother
for swim lessons. They lived in a mansion with a big pool
in the Hollywood hills. For seven weeks I clung to the edge,
or walked in the shallow end.
I had a crush on Cheryl, but she went for Ross Schwartz,
whose father produced *Gilligan's Island* and the *Brady Bunch*.

The Schwartzes lived on Fryman Place, near Gene Autry's ranch
and Mickey Rooney's bungalow. I was the son of a car mechanic.
I was afraid of water. Cheryl's mother said I'd never swim.

Trying to impress a girl in college, I dove into an Olympic pool,
thrashed to the end, pulled myself onto the coping,
and threw up.

Instead of swimming now, I float on my back in seawater.
I wear glasses so I can have the sky and the other bathers.
In my seventy-fifth year, I came to Cheryl Vitarelli's house in a dream.
Her house was more Mayan temple than Hollywood.
Her mother greeted me, shook my hand warmly,
saying she'd hoped that my life had gone well.
Yes, I said, I am a person who floats over great depths,
the fins of yellow fish, and the backs of turtles.

IN STAIRWELLS

"The wide 'comma' between the ring finger
and middle finger of your left hand
will limit your career as a concert guitarist,"
my teacher, Oscar Giglia, told me when I was twelve.
For ten years afterward, I believed him.
For the next twenty, I tried workarounds,
slowing difficult passages, changing fingerings,
listening to each note-strike emanate into space.
But I still only played in stairwells after work,
in closed bedrooms, empty warehouses.
After forty years, the comma itself
began to release sounds.
As I listened, I learned how to play
from a stillness under the strings.
Notes came shyly at first, then like cliff swallows.

LINEAGE

I began teaching my son guitar when he was eleven,
the same age I'd begun.
By seventeen, he could play scales faster than the speed of thinking,
and Bach with a feel from some place already deep in his future.

I gave him my rosewood and spruce Manuel de la Chica guitar
that vibrated when he breathed, and smelled of the stones of Granada.

Then my son studied with a master, Evangelos, in Athens,
who said, "Your playing will carry you into old age."

After that, he apprenticed to a Gypsy with terrible teeth,
whose playing name was "The Rabbit of Cartagena"—
for his speed and leaps. He played in small plazas for beer.

Now my son teaches guitar to undocumented immigrant kids
who somehow made it from Central America to Oakland.
He and I play duets. I take the easier parts.

THE NATURAL HISTORY OF VACANT LOTS

The weeds emigrate from Europe, Asia, South America
and root here in Oakland. Chicory, pimpernel, flax, dock.
Lots permit nonhuman strangers. A feral kitten
hears a leaky pipe and takes a drink. Night herons roost.
Rats run along broken walls. Mostly, lots are overlooked,
walked by for years. How many people stop to watch
the rank profusion? Lots go on anyway.
Buildings go up and down, lots persist.
Small and incidental patches of the beginning.
My Yiddish-speaking grandmother Rose
became demented at eighty. Spoke a gibberish
that sounded like Tagalog. Sometimes I could reach
a sweet leftover part of her that looked quizzically,
smiled, then put its hard blue lips to my cheek.

FERAL CATS

Unmanageable, spurting out
of trash bins all over the Levant.
They make maddening mating noises.
Joel says they killed off warblers
in the North East. Cats carry parasites
and viruses, although their brains
are folded like ours. One found me
in Jerusalem. I was sure it was the food
I brought out to the porch.
After she'd feed, she'd come over
to rub my leg and talk.
My wife hated the little bitch.
It's the cat or me. What could I say?
I kept trying to hide my relationship,
but the animal would call every mid-day.
If I said that I'd looked deeply
into her gold eyes, and that the cat
had looked back steadily into my eyes,
my wife would have thought I was insane,
or worse. But it was queer and profound.
An absolute truth I could never prove.

WHEN I WAS BORN

my father was twenty-one and just out of the Navy.
A mechanic's hands, tough hazel eyes.
What could he do with a baby?
What could he do with his twelve-year old boy
who listened to madrigals and read alone?
My father wanted a doctor or an athlete for a son.
After he died, I found the passionate, worried, funny, literate letters
between him and a woman my mother and I didn't know about.
"You are my Jewish giant." "Write me tomorrow—it's been a week"
"Can we meet in Ohio?" "Who were the guys playing cards with you?"
I only had a few hints of his inner life while I was growing up:
how his eyes filled to the lids, but not over them,
when his childhood friend, Melvin, drowned;
when he cranked up the stereo he built from scratch.
There must have been a whole wet cavern hidden in his chest
filled with flowstone, columns, curtains, corals, pillars.
I am my father. I am not my father.

HIS BODY DOES NOT LIE

A cranky lizard doing pushups
on a chunk of greywacke sandstone.
Pulsing body—shingled, cracked.
Leaf-like hands—veiny, ribbed.
Hot in heat, cold in thaw—this lizard is like iron.
Mostly left alone. Overlooked.
Quick to shadows. Hiding in nettles.
Beneath the throat a scarlet gland betrays him.

THE BEGINNING

Started smoking weed, listening to jazz, Wilson Pickett, Otis Redding.
Jammed blues guitar every night. Got busy being in love with Laura.
Slid behind on the freshman assignments. Tried to catch up
by combining many topics into one paper.
Edmund Burke, Freud, plus Euripides.
The Federalists, Malcolm X, plus Lear.
Organized them by lining quote-cards up on the floor, then shuffling.
At the end of term, I gave a recital of the music I'd been playing
instead of doing the assignments. Bach's Prelude and Fugue in D major.
A Dowland fantasia. A Couperin passacaglia.
Professor Tussman said that I was slovenly but talented,
that he recognized my synthetic mind, an evident delight,
and that he would have flunked me but for the Bach.

COMING CLEAN

I've lied on my resume.
Said I was a music major instead of poly sci.
Added a year to one job to cover my having been fired.
Lied about feeding the poor at the Midnight Mission.
I've also lied to people's faces.
I couldn't believe such bullshit was coming out of my mouth.
I was a student of Segovia. My family escaped the Nazis to Shanghai.
Immediately after, I'd tell myself that what I said was true enough.
I'd bounce between belief and disbelief like AC current.
Until I came to rest on self-hate. I wanted to tell them I'd lied,
that I was simply a regular person without tinsel or colored lights.
But it seemed too late. Now I look over what my life really is.
How it is sufficient, despite itself.

INTROVERSION

I try to keep up with a woman in sweatpants steaming up the mountain.
She is thirty years younger. I finally yield to the limit of my lungs
and watch her disappear into a switchback. Slowed down,
I find clusters of ruby berries, umbels of yampah
floating above hissing seas of wild oats.
I've preferred to move quietly through the woods,
letting phenomena stab me into memory.
Light glancing off pine
racks me into the Franklin Canyon of my boyhood.
The odor of crushed black sage is what I masturbated to in Cold Creek
as hawks rode thermals above me. The bouncing call of a wrentit
is my childhood grace, for to hear it meant I was alone,
unmolested on the hill behind my house.
I don't like to see other people on the mountain,
though I say Hello and step off the trail to let them pass.
I've even hidden myself in brush to avoid possibly pleasant encounters.
I pick the hottest days and the steepest trails in order to cut the chances.
In this privacy, I can talk myself into selves I never imagined.

INSTRUCTIONS TO THE PLAYER

Despacio. Slow. *Legato.* Smooth.
Listen carefully for the overtones,
how each note spreads upward in tissues of dissonance.
Feel the music enter your hands.
Take speed only as the curves of sound allow.
Hear birds of the season
inside the fragrant woods of your guitar:
sparrow, wren, hawk, flicker. It must be summer.
Cottonwood, pine, oak, alder—
each given voice by the wind through your fingers.
You become the fugue itself, a chant, a plainsong,
a man slowly walking his music to a mountain ridge
where he can hear for fifty years,
in consort with cloud and sky.

HEAT DOME, 116 DEGREES

Heat flenses my back.
Melts cartilage, softens muscle.
I'm nauseous.
The egg of noon cracks,
its hot yolk leaking on my face.
My son pours water on my neck,
holds my head while I puke.
We laugh. We're the only idiots
on Mount Diablo today.
My son does not do
the thing his young body easily could do:
run upslope lightly as a deer.
Instead he fusses over his father.
He'd like to move to Madrid, he tells me.
But I know that he's staying here
because of his mother and me
and will leave only when we're dead.
I finally stand up, using sticks.
He walks behind me,
keeping his pace with my shuffle.

NAVARRO POINT

The cream-colored mother seal and her pup lie next to each other
on a black-sand beach protected from the pelagic sea by reef.
The tiny pup pushes into his mother's belly nudging for her nipples.
The mother is exhausted, I imagine, because of the search for fish
and the constant feeding of the baby. Where is the father?
The seals seem interested in the people who watch them from the cliff-top,
tipping their heads up when they hear voices above the wave-sounds.
One of the on-lookers throws a stick down at the seals,
which somehow hits the mother, who lumbers quickly
to push her pup toward water. They slide into a sheltered pool,
swim around a rock, then out into the surf, disappearing in froth.
I say nothing to the man.
When the Russians, Finns, and New Englanders
were trapping here in the nineteenth century,
they stacked seal hides ten-feet high.
Now the coastline appears wild and the seals have come back.
I see corpses.

WITH HANDS TIED BEHIND MY BACK

Ten thousand years ago the last mastodon roasted
when glaciers moved away.
Now the oaks are heat-stressed,
weakened by beetle, killed by fungus.
I like living here, on earth, despite the heat.
And because there are things like the Iris Society,
which gives blue ribbons for the best tall bearded flower.
The modern world is computers, violence, fragments.
But the passacaglia I play in my stairwell after work
rearranges my cells into slow stately processions.
Thus altered, I can see color again.
The orange-bellied, olive-brown newt
crunching over leaves to her mating pool—
I find her by accident,
the way anything important gets found.
By next year, the pool will be gone.

I LEARNED TO TAKE CARE AT THE END

Was it in sixth grade, or seventh? I remember a biology test,
questions about frogs, or mollusks, or the water cycle of plants.
Did I hear the advice from a teacher, or discover it on my own:
Slow down for the last questions, making sure not to get cocky at the end.
I said to myself, "Read carefully now, here's where you'll trip."
Years later I saw the movie version of *Death of a Salesman*.
Judy Garland said, "Care must be taken, attention must be paid."
I hear her on a steep downhill on the last part of a hike.
I've had many falls just there.
The big fall is close. I must be very careful.
Leaving nothing out.

JULIAN MUDGE, CLASSICAL GUITARIST, LONDON, 1971

The green apples Rusty brought today for lunch summon you, Julian.
They are like the good ones you'd buy at the greengrocer
that sounded high and clear when you snapped them
with a flick of your middle finger.
I summon your hands from the long curving spears
of the green aloe plant on my desk.
I summon you from the Hotel de Cluny's room with one bed,
which three guitarists shared on our adventures in Paris.
After London, we went back to our home countries.
You died, Julian, somewhere in the late middle of our lives.
I heard from your sister that you had played on,
amid the groves of your father's apples.
I played on, in the dusk stairwells of my many offices,
the Bach Cello Suite you transcribed for me fifty years ago.

MAPPING TIME

We call it the "tarantula trail"
because we've found them here, for decades.
They dig burrows into the fine sand
that sloughs off the cliff-face.
Their hairiness scares me,
as do their eyes and sperm-laden pedipalps.
My son doesn't mind spiders,
and he takes photos to show his friends.
He does hate the snakes we find on the "snake trail,"
where, every spring, rattler babies squirm
out of the family's winter nest.
The manzanitas on the "manzanita-barrens trail"
have suffered a die-off. Heat killed them.
The Coulter pines on the "pine trail"
have baked to fine, dry lace.
The "chanterelle trail"—
which runs through a copse of oaks—
has yielded nothing during these five years of drought.
We keep coming back to all our trails
to find whatever we are given to find.
Today, besides the spider, it's two yellow-throated warblers
and a rank Jimson weed with white trumpet-flowers.
We like that the Volvon Indians figured out how to make
an hallucinogenic decoction without killing themselves,
while also tipping their minds into cosmic time.
Our time is his thirty-four years on this wide earth.

TRESPASSER

A grove of first-growth *Sequoia sempervirens* quiets my voice,
rearranges my molecules with volatile scents and palpable greens.
These trees have so far lasted through the whole of the human atrocity
without moving. Most were unwounded, or, if wounded,
managed to live on with burnt cores.

In an evergreen grove, sound hollows and expands.
I expand within.
Humors that have abided in me since I was a boy
sweep me gusting into the trees.

The grove was named for a lumber baron, Mr. Hendy.
I am a tourist in this remnant
it pleased him to keep for his own.
As I walk amid sword ferns and sorrel,
a deer streaks
through bronze columns.

HERMIT OAK

On a hillside, having defeated younger trees,
it stands alone.
Bark, thick-fissured; girth, elephantine;
lobe-leaved; wounded and scarred;
caves where limbs were;
branches tortuose, gnarled.
As it has done for three hundred years,
it greens in April:
down-covered leaves, silky catkins.
I've rested alone against its trunk for thirty years,
sluices of shadows raining down on my head.

FIELD STUDY IN JANUARY

The Coulter pine tree that my son began to climb
when he was ten—and kept climbing for the next twenty years—
turned to rust and powder this year, weeping amber sap,
needle-clusters fossilized. The mushroom patches
that yielded themselves to us for thirty years
disappeared this dry fall. Plum and almond trees
that used to bloom in March, now blossom in winter.
My son and I come upon some cattle who will be meat.
A curious one with brown-black hide and wet nose walks over.
My son holds out a handful of sparse, sere winter grass.
The animal takes. Its breathing is large and hollow.
Its lungs will be filled with smoke by June.

IF YOU CAN'T HUM IT, YOU CAN'T PLAY IT

That's why we hear Glenn Gould singing off key
on the famous recording of the Goldberg Variations.
Giving them shape and sway as he played them.
The arc between the voice in the mind
and the long finger-bones, vibrating in sympathy,
is where music happens. If there is no
music that is ours alone, already, and silent,
keeping us company, giving us meaning,
then what? When I look at the wet lawn
in Snow Park, I see the geese glide down
heavy before they are there.

ON A CLEAR DAY

All my seventy-five years are pressed
into an afternoon here at Heather Farms pond.
I'm blown by north winds from high desert mesas.
Geese mostly peacefully float on the pond, clean themselves, dip,
rack their wings, gobble and trumpet.
Some sleep for a minute or two, resting their heads
backwards in the cleft between folded wings.
A mallard pair enters—the iridescent green-necked one,
his brownish mate. Coots. Egrets, both Great and Snowy.
Next to the pond is an ancient valley oak
with cracked and harrowed trunk.
Hundreds of its branches twist and jut.
On a distant playground, balls thump, kids scream.
I am not old. I am not young.
The wind picks up the dry leaves
and spins them in circles.

FANTASIA NO. 26

The deer browse willow, oak, poplar in the woods near my house.
When they hear me talk, they stop, turn their long faces, then canter off.
This afternoon, on my porch, I'm playing Milán's *fantasia* on the guitar.
Sixteenth-century music mixing with the whoosh of vulture wings, wind,
scents of the hayfield. One deer stops. Listens. Stays.
Is there surprise in its eyes? In mine?
When I stop playing, it steps, leisurely, away into the grove.

LISTEN

He was not a natural. It came hard.
An odd student, he wanted most to be alone,
in fields, olive groves, mountains.
Some say he fell into mastery of the deep song by pure luck.
Now he's old. His runs are uneven, rhythms awkward.
Hands mistake-ridden, sometimes stiffening to claws.
He is the greatest guitarist in Cartagena.
He sings, out of torn lungs,
the music of clouds rushing past a burning moon.

MY BLOODLINE

My great-uncle Maxie was imprisoned three years at San Quentin.
His booking sheet noted his "color" as "Jew."
My great-grandfather Mendel-Yehuda Liftman—
who burned down his slum buildings for the insurance money—
was the *moyl* who circumcised my father, cousins, grandfathers,
uncles, most Jews of Chelsea, Everett, and Malden,
and, when he was in his late nineties, me.
Great-uncle Al imprisoned in Boston for selling *traif* meat as kosher.
My father Len (Moishe-Leyb) had a forty-year affair with TV's Lois Lane.
She visited him in the cancer ward when my mother left for the day.
I (Hayyim-Shia) shoplifted books, cans of crabmeat, whole steaks
and hid them in my booster pockets. I began to play music in secret.
No one in my genealogical line was a doctor, architect, scholar, lawyer.
Many of the men were criminals, or too lazy to be.
I wonder about the people who do the tests
and find out they are tenth cousins of Mozart.
Ralph Waldo Emerson III lived across the street from us in Hollywood.
He married Dodo Dewey, Admiral Dewey's great-granddaughter.
They had a Tiki Bar. They were nice to me and my sister.
Doctors removed his brain tumor. He never read Emerson.
All my cousins who remained in Igumen and Odessa
after the Nazis invaded were shot into the ditches
they themselves were forced to dig.

SHTETL LIFE

One trunk with two dresses, pearls to buy passage,
a siddur, photos of dead relatives.
You flee Minsk for Hamburg, then America.
A month of nausea and heaves.
You hold the head of your little brother Avrumke.
Hold your older sister, Brokhe, who sobs daily
about her being raped by the river.
Arrive in Boston still a teenager.
Meet Izzy, your second cousin, your husband-to-be.
Bake apples, fish, noodles, chickens.
In a pistachio and cream colored shop on Beacon Street,
you become a corsetiere to the Boston Brahmins.
Suffer backaches, fevers, miscarriages.
See doctors who have no idea.
Finally, you show. Give birth to your first child at home.
Your second child dies age seven months.
Husband dies suddenly, but doctors have no idea.
Every year you celebrate Rosh Hashanah
and the birthdays of Al and Bessie,
the new names of Avrumke and Brokhe.
The rest of the year you are in mourning.
You live to eighty-seven, dying at home after a short fever.
Your daughter, my mother, lives to 2011.
I remember the feel of the black shift-ball of my Ford
after I said goodbye to you when I went away to college.
How I bruised my palm squeezing it.

BIRDS FILL MY JERUSALEM GARDEN

I know them a little, only by their different squawks and songs.
They flash through so quickly.
I can't name them—I'm a stranger here.
One, with black hood and crest, rests in the pepper tree,
giving me time to look him up: bulbul.
The garden's walls do not keep anything out that is borne by air:
wind; neighbors' voices in languages I don't understand—
some days anger, some days gossip; distant singing or hollering mobs;
the violin of a Russian immigrant in the next building.
In the afternoon, light is stained by the many greens of the Levant.
Sitting amid the sounds and the light, I watch a black cat
stalk a lizard in the uncut grass, grass as tall—
I suddenly remember—as grew from my mother's unmarked grave.

LUIS DE MILÁN

Lived in Renaissance Spain after the Reconquista.
He composed for the court. Was adept at the *vihuela*,
a lovely, quiet, early guitar, shaped like a young torso.
He was also a poet. He titled his book *El Maestro*.
I began playing the six easy *pavanas* when I was thirteen.
They felt square, with block-like chords.
When I was seventeen, I undertook the difficult *fantasias*—
combinations of simple modal chant-lines
and running embellishments in marvelous variations.
I didn't understand them for the next fifty years.
When I turned seventy, I slowed them down.
Allowed them. He wrote, *Now there came a wind*.

OLD CLOTHES

Ties too wide and too paisley;
fake cashmere scarves I bought on 5th Avenue;
suits too small and of the wrong style;
denim shirts I wore in college.
I keep them all.
They cushion my being;
hold my human odor in moth-eaten cloth;
remind me of the years of standing in court;
of sweating up steep canyon bottoms;
of feeling her hands on my worsted pant-legs.
They are like the photos in my attic
that mean nothing to anybody else.
I've seen whole hoarder-houses drained of crap in two days.
My son will call *Got Junk?* after I'm dead.
I've already apologized to him
for the drawers of fingernail clippings,
thousands of poems, stashed porn,
shocks he'll find in my computer.
I see how a person accumulates over a lifetime,
building ornate shells around the soft parts.
Like Decorator Crabs,
sticking seaweed and bits of broken shell
onto their carapaces in order to hide.

STILL, A RICHNESS

The Lebanese part of my family, the Kahlils, fed me *Kibbeh nayyeh*—
raw ground lamb, cracked wheat *burghul*, olive oil, raw onions.
Sahtain! my uncle Joe would yell when we sat for supper. *Double health!*
Aunt Laila read my coffee grounds in upturned cups.
Stevie, you'll meet a woman with large breasts, she foretold.
Aunt Cora made a Ouija board out of a marble slab,
which predicted I'd make a clam sauce
that would drive women to my bed.
The aunts ran an electrolysis center
to remove the middle parts of eyebrows.
Uncle Joe got into the Boston Mafia,
along with Irish, Italian, Jewish, and Arab gangsters.
I waited tables at the family's restaurant, *The Prophet*,
while the mobsters played cards in the back room and plotted.
My uncle would make me lie on the floor of his coupe
when he delivered satchels of cash.
Once I saw a little snubnose revolver still smoking in his huge hand.
Joe played Ella Fitzgerald's "Autumn Leaves" for me on his stereo.
I learned the color blue.

THE GREAT CENTRAL VALLEY

From brisk-running, to soggy-slow, to mud-caked—
the irrigation canal's flow varies by season.
When there's water moving in spring,
egrets—both great and snowy—
wade on twiggy black legs,
spearing minnows and chubs.
In summer, it's only horse-flies.
I usually walk the canal bank slowly.
Today I am running.
Everything is different in speed's bliss.
The hymn says: There is a book
that only those who run may read.

REINCARNATION

I was an Irish peasant who died at forty-one in the mid-19th century.
I was married, in County Cork, to a girl with green eyes
and swan's-down hair. After my death, I remained in the ether
for a century, bodiless and homeless.
My grandfather's sperm and my grandmother's egg united in Odessa.
He was a thief and philanderer.
She took revenge with a lover in the hat shop.
My father was born, became a thief and philanderer in turn.
My mother took revenge by denying him sex and studying psychology.
I was born nonetheless, studied Hebrew, became a poet.
Certain Jews believe in gilgul—transmigration of souls
from body to body over time and space. I know that I was an Irishman
because I sing Irish songs I never learned, love Irish girls I never met.
After my death I'll probably incarnate as a squirrel.
I have real affinity for them—always escaping dogs.
As I age, I find myself rubbing my forehead often.
Am I polishing something?
It is a small jewel, and it defies degradation,
pulsing through my lifetimes.
The jewel is flawed, cracked, impure.
Light catches in it.

MUSIC FROM THE NEXT ROOM

A boy is playing strict exercises on the piano.
Now he begins to improvise.
Takes off into a transparent morning,
tufts of grass, big sky.
In his brown eyes and small hands,
this music comes *back*,
a slender cord, from his future.
He exceeds himself in this foreshadowed manhood.
How fine it must be for him, out there.

THE PENIS

It is a gathering and a history,
fuming here in my hand,
containing the ashes of the Jews of Naples,
philosophers, farmers, plantsmen.
The Lord made something
to be smoked, and I am smoking it.

ALL OF IT

In Heather Farms Park, three children run through the beds of old roses.
I'm reading on my bench about bonobos in the Congo.
The ice cream truck plays "Pop Goes the Weasel" continuously.
I take in bonobo orgasms and the mentation inside my brain—
all conjuring a psychic stylus that composes a symphony,
dissonant, drum-charged,
with moments of accidental harmony.
A Garden of Old Roses is something *extra* in this world.
Brief music amid the catastrophe.

PROCLAMATION

WHEREAS the oldest junipers on Mount Diablo are twisted,
scorched, frozen, starved on pulverized chert.
Bark: shredded. Leaves: scale-like. Color: dragon-green—

AND WHEREAS the leaves of younger junipers are needle-like,
which, when I crush them between the thumb and forefinger
of my plant-crushing hand, have little scent and a thin bluish-gray color—

AND WHEREAS, when I crush the leaves of the ancient juniper
I've known for thirty years on a slope in Oat Canyon,
the scent released is of time and experience distilled
into a rounded sharpness that spirits me instantly
across seventy years to my grandmother's bedroom,
the sour odors of her powders and unguents—

NOW, THEREFORE, by all men presents, I aver:
The oldest is best, holding, as it does,
the risen juice of the earth.

IT'S ALL IN THE INCIDENTALS

I have no love for baseball.
My father never taught me how to play,
and I suffered Little League
with undiagnosed bad eyes.
I did admire the Dodger shortstop, Maury Wills,
the greatest base-stealer,
who'd pump his legs before exploding toward second base.
I also liked the man in the next seat who sat quietly with his cigar,
letting the ash build up until it fell on his pants.
I craved the first brilliance
after coming out of the tunnel into the stadium.
I was puzzled by the Chavez Ravine neighborhood
we drove through to get there:
Families giving stink-eyes to cars of fans.
Even then I knew the sadness of baseball.
The way our neighbor Vic listened
to the twilight games through his earpiece,
while the kids and wife ate supper.
And in the way the exuberance of the game
didn't follow me back into our den,
decorated with colored glass, fishnet floats,
and tiki torches burning around the wet bar.

OAKLAND SCRAP METAL

Forklifts move pallets of aluminum, stainless, copper.
The scrappers pay cash for stolen metals.
I'm alone here, as unnoticed as I'd be in the woods.
Around me are city plants, growing through cracks:
natives, invasives, aliens.
Fescue, cheeseweed, henbit, sowthistle, fleabane.

Across the way, on the roof of Tin's Tea House—
a gang of five black-crowned night herons,
with their Qing Dynasty feather hats and orange eyes.
They are serious trouble, scuffling around, stooped and splay-footed.
Even crows won't compete for the garbage Tin puts out.
I like the countryside more, but this is what I have.

Does my afternoon at the scrap yard help me survive my job?
Yes, in the same way that music heard in the mind,
while I'm waiting for a green light, makes the sirens bearable.

MY FATHER

"I am dead."
Yes, Dad, I saw how cancer dug into all the dirty places.
I was there when you pulled out the oxygen cannula from your nose,
then turned to the wall for your final breaths—gravelly trumpetings—
the same way, maybe, that you spat out notes from the brass bell
of your coronet in the Everett High band.
I saw your eyes gel, legs stop thrashing.
I heard you say in your delirium
that you didn't want to go to the Hot Place.
I called the mortuary and saw them strap you to a gurney.
I shoveled dirt on your linen-wrapped body.

This morning, I crank up the 1812 Overture for you—
it was your favorite to play on those few times
when you felt success as a young father—
waves of orchestral forces, cannon shots, cathedral bells.
You, who had slept my childhood away on your couch,
wake up, alive, brave—before the music stops.

SOME COOKING MISTAKES ARE SPIRITUAL NOT TECHINCAL

My grandmother made her fried *kreplach* tiny and golden.
They shone with chicken fat, rich in light and salt.
So what if *kreplach* shorten a life by a year or two?
Almost all cooking in any generation fails.
Because the cooks fall fast into narrowing chutes of style.
Only a few cooks make food worth living or dying for,
which they owe to their mothers, who preserved and taught
the taste of a Carpathian paradise—
barley, mushrooms, birch, larch, meadows, a cow.
These are the lucky ones—
stumbling, useless in commerce, barred from markets of exchange.
Saved into kitchens.
Building their bread with yeast, water, salt, groats.
Sometime—between my first two jobs as a new lawyer—
I lost the recipe cards she'd given me—
written in Yiddish in a rough hand.

ONIONS

I don't remember how I fell into eating raw onions.
Was it my grandmother's fried potato and onion *latkes*?
Or Uncle Joe's *kibbeh nayyeh*—raw ground lamb, oil, bulgur, onions?
In elementary school, one of the girls said, "You stink."
After that, I never ate onions before school.
At dusk, I'd lie back on the warm hood of the Pontiac,
eat an onion like an apple, and watch the stars,
trillions of buds in rounded umbels shining with allium-milk.
As an adult, I didn't give up eating onions.
I'd take a swig of whisky before I'd kiss a woman.
I'd gulp Listerine before I'd go to court.
Onions comfort me. The way masturbation does.
My own two sharp pleasures.
I am careful now to talk at an angle in meetings.
I gave up raw onions once, for a while,
when I first was in love with Elena, in my twenties.
I showered for her twice a day. Her husband discovered us
before our affair matured enough for me to start eating onions again.
She remembers me as sweet-breathed.

DIG

Dig anywhere in the fields of Belarus and Ukraine—
bones and onions rise though the clods.
Bones of my ancestors. Food of my ancestors,
fertilized by blood, urine, lime, offal.
When I bite through the dry parchment-skin of the onion,
the first taste is bitter,
but the deeper I eat, the sweeter it grows.
Dug from common dirt, common food.
Dug from common dirt, common bones.
In spring, I eat the flowers of wild onions:
sparklers detonate my mouth.
I have a sepia photo of my great-great grandfather,
Eliyahu Botwinik, rabbi, Hebrew teacher, Master of Onions.
His bones are in a grave he was forced to dig
before the mobile killing unit shot him in the head.
Onions sprout from his toes.

ONIONS FROM ANTIQUITY TO NOW

Archaeologists discovered traces of onions
in the eye sockets of Ramesses's mummy.
The onion's spherical shape and concentric rings
symbolized, for the Egyptians, eternal life.

Pliny the Elder found carbonized onions in Pompeii.
He cited the onion's medicinal properties:
cure for eyesores, toothaches, bad breath, dog bites, lumbago.

The onion of the Jews of Eastern Europe
descended from the ancestral, wild onion of the Levant.
My great-great-great grandmother's winter onions were bitter,
but grew sweet in the cooking. Each carp and chicken
was beautified by the pearly fan-shaped swathes of onion,
their fleshy leaves enveloping the central buds.

Today, I eat my onion raw,
which leaves me radically simplified:
I can't breathe around people.
So I go for a walk alone on Mount Diablo
where I find the wild, magenta, sickle-leaf onions
that explode in my mouth.

ANNALS OF ODESSA, 1891

"Why should I buy more food for you?
You'll only eat it."

THE TERRAIN

I cut chain-links guarding the weedlot of my crotch.
Crawl under barbed fences shielding the creek in my navel.
Go deeper into the urban waste of my chest.
I'm on the hunt for cracked iron pipes in the valley behind my liver.
Am I able to follow the crackle of shorted electric cables to my heart?
I chase the half-wild fox into my mouth.
My hands bruise from pulling open the sluice gates of my ribs.
I hear the many tones of steel as I beat the stanchions around my throat.
As I walk the transepts of my body, I feel its incidental sensoria.
At last, I recognize instincts by their odors.
In the spontaneous flux and confusion of my pioneering breaths is joy.
How easy it suddenly seems to open the shutters of my ears and eyes
to the dawn chorus of birds.

SARABANDE, SUITE FOR UNACCOMPANIED CELLO, J.S. BACH

Piece by piece the rococo facade
taken down, ripped back
to bricks and iron.
Smoke blown off the yellow pine-flame.
The farm as mud and cows.
I'm walking the same streets
I walked when I was young.
Maybe I'm indistinguishable
from the darling who hungered
for compliments and fashioned
his pleasing style. I'm in plain
pants and shirt, walking alone.
Alive after years of getting
rich and sad, then poor
and sad, burned clean.
Sturdy and shivering
in the moonlight.

LEO OPPENHEIMER

I summon you out of your truffles and hazelnut paste,
cordials with spears of sugar in brandy, cat's tongues, violet drops—
fashioned according to recipes you brought out of the Camps
and took to East 14th Street in Oakland.
But your real genius was the *invented* candies.
Smoothing warm chocolate on marble,
spreading it like impasto, you watched for secret signs—
a thin film, a temperature you checked on your inner wrist,
the way a mother feels the milk for her baby—
the exact moment to add the cacao and butter.
Then you'd mix and wait for the slight odor that meant now.
Raspberries. Burnt filberts. Orange peels.
And the swift sculpting of some excess never to be sold.
You created candy no *bonbonniere* ever dreamed of.
Tarot decks in mocha,
a fleet of German warships,
Zeus and Hephaestus in apricot,
Aphrodite in slab-simple chocolate.
Now you make one up, Stevie. Surprise me.
And I'd try. It was our delight.
We'd spread our candy on the cooling table,
our mouths smeared with pleasure,
your spirit rising like all the flowers of Switzerland.
You knew I'd never be a *bonbonniere*.
In the cool mornings, before I go to my law office,
I step out, smelling the wind, looking for colors.

LISTENING FOR THE FAINT TONES

Must music be heard?
Food must be eaten, and anyone
else's always tastes better
than my lonely-man supper
of raw onions and a little meat.
I hear loneliness, and I hum it
to myself. This separation
from the world must be
the beginning of death, I think,
as I watch two young women,
gurgling and laughing
like spring-fed brooks,
two benches over.
Every day I wait, almost
content, terribly aching.

THE GENTLE ART OF SWEDISH DEATH CLEANING

The man in line at Safeway held the book.
I thought it must be about the Swedish way of washing the body.
As Jews wash a body while reciting Psalms and other verses—
Your belly—golden wheat adorned with daffodils.
The Swedes must do their death-cleaning in an immaculate room,
with simple lighting fixtures and modern tables.
After which, I imagine, they take rapid shots of Aquavit.
The way Jews take Slivovitz or Kirsch.
Jews provide the careful cleaning as part of a Holy Society—
volunteers who are expert at dealing with corpses and souls.
The body is guarded, not leaving it alone like a useless vessel.
This is a high privilege.
I have tended the bodies of my father and one poet.
The only path though it for me was to remember the way
I'd wash my baby son in his bassinet.
When I googled the Safeway man's book in order to buy it,
I found out it was about cleaning up your clutter
before you die, so your children won't have to do it.
Also a holy office.

FULFILLMENT

In the dark den with knotty pine paneling, they are bickering.
Every day. Their ten-year-old boy shuts his eyes.
As afternoons darken to dusk, father sleeps on the couch.
Mother applies the putty of evening to her face.
The boy goes to his room to open his eyes
to what he saw on a field trip: dancers spiral-dancing in flowering grass
to a music that was seeds lit by midsummer lightning.
Sky throbbing. The boy moves each night further into his future,
as he follows the faint sound of a violin
coming to him from behind a stone wall.
He will learn how to find the gate
that opens into a garden.

THE SHADOW OF MY SHADOW

Inside my chest is Filippo Ciccarelli,
with silk ties and broken thumbs
some fellows gave him for being too happy.
He loves everything and keeps pushing
his insane chatter into my mouth.
Makes me kiss all the guests
and gush enthusiasm over them.
Is he so insincere?
It's not just meat for my inner Italian.
It's *This steak is alive!*
Not just sky for him. But sky the violet
of Umbrian mushrooms.
The best Naples. The most beautiful.
The softest. The wind inside the wind
sweetened by every flower and pine
on the Amalfi coast.
The sea of the sea.
The stone of the stone.
People think they're just exaggerations.
I used to think so too.
But here's my Filippo,
pretending he's Caruso,
pouring out his sorrow
in the yellow kitchen,
noodles drying on the chairs.

GOATS KEEP

a small distance between themselves.
The goatherd calls that distance "courtesy."
Goats have slit pupils, as do cats and snakes.
Their eyes are the visible shadow I worry is inside them, in me.
Goats will walk past spring grass and flowers
to browse on gorse, thorny burnet, spiny spurge.
Goatherds in Greece put bells on their goats,
which I imagine is to keep devils away.
One summer on the island of Paros
I played a sarabande on guitar
to a group of goats eating willow leaves.
They kept eating.
One, with leaves dangling from her black lips, came near,
looking at me with those eyes, for what seemed like minutes,
then skittered away when I stopped.

FOR TWENTY YEARS

"I see life as it is," Tom said, telling me about fists,
thrown bottles, meth, crank, early deaths.
When I'd go to see his punk band, The Toiling Midgets,
he'd stay close, before and after the sets, guarding me from violence.
During, he'd buy me a Pabst Blue Ribbon and sit me on the side,
away from mosh pits of scars barely healed, cuts newly opened.

Tom built a Japanese gateway to the garden of our friendship,
hand-cut from sugi and cedar. He used fine steel and bronze saws,
knives, chisels. He shingled it with hammered hinoki bark.
The gate glowed with moss. We held it up together.
After Tom died, I couldn't manage alone.
The gate fell into a deep pool, gold and mottled carp
floating over the hidden wreck.

ABSOLUTE SCALE

I grew up in pure sunlight, green lawns,
with the particular birds of a hot chaparral,
under shady cottonwoods and sycamores,
amid odors of laurel, sage, walnut, sumac.
It was against those loose, imprecise things
that I would measure everything after.
Paris and London did not smell like grass
crisped in the summer heat of Hollywood.
New York lacked the colors to penetrate my retinas.
Just as Suzanne, in high school, was the measure
of every mouth and mind I was to love
until I married Marcia.
After I wept hearing it at thirteen,
Monteverdi's *Lasciatemi morire*
was the gauge for all feeling in music.
Everywhere is either a *punctum*
into the sweet orange groves of adolescence,
or a mere study of interesting features.
It is not that the places detached
from the magnitude are less fine.
It is that they are nothing.

FEASTS IN THE BRONZE AGE
Israel Museum

A terra cotta cultic vessel of 3000 B.C.E depicts musicians
playing double-flutes of clay and bone,
seven-stringed harps, rattles, finger-cymbals, tambours.
I sit on the museum bench and imagine my fingers plucking
a proto-lute made of gut strings stretched across a tortoise shell.
My songs would be joyful and melancholy.
What did their songs sound like? What words?
They must have been about death, and the brief music before.

LAWYER

I stole time from billable hours to play guitar in the stairwell.
The music reached from Oakland to the enclosed gardens of Andalucia.
As I grew older, judges grew younger.
They listened to me. Maybe it was the music they heard.
I do not envy other lawyers, the rich ones,
except for my occasional phantasies about a house in Malibu.
They wanted that, and they have it.
I wanted something different.
Music saved my death.

THE MAN THINKS

that after seventy-five years his life
lacks life.
His life is dead.
He chops onions with his best knife,
careful not to cut himself this time.
The slices get thinner and thinner,
translucent, finally not existing.
The man first heard "my life is dead" as a passing thought.
It stuck.
What is he to do, now that he knows?
He doesn't want another life.
He's been rattling around his empty house,
which is his mind, for years, except for the few small animals
that passed through on occasion:
the cat that draped itself over the man's neck
when the man studied law;
the house finches and sparrows bickering at the feeder.
Will the man live through this death?
He won't leave life, not wanting to burden his family
with the cleanup. Do nothing, he thinks.
Move nothing.
Let death move over him, going any way it does.
Lie back on the backyard grass.
Let clouds fill the sky from the west.
Let wind carry them beyond him.

ACKNOWLEDGMENTS

Suzan: my sister and my witness.

Rusty Morrison: my friend and partner in the art.

Laura Joakimson and Sharon Zetter: my book-shepherds.

Harvey Malloy: my brother in the guitar.

Larry Felson: my brother in the art.

Jack Gilbert z"l; Joe Smith; Mike Jones; Mike Edwards; Donald Brees; Barry Tagrin; Audrey King; Tia Ballentine; Lexi Potter; Liza Flum; Ken Keegan z"l; C.S. Giscombe; Tom Mallon z"l; Nancie Lualhati; Thom, Virgil and Francis McCorgray-Mallon; Amy Thomas; John Beebe; Linda Elkin; Richard Silberg; Joyce Jenkins; Lucille Lang Day; Jim LeCuyer; Tony Keppelman; Lisa Rappoport; Bill Mayer z"l; Laura Lane; John Goodman.

Some of these poems published in *Hayden's Ferry Review*, *Marsh Hawk*, *Genesis West*, *Sporklet*, *Periodicities*.

STEVEN ROOD was born in Los Angeles, attended Hollywood High School and U.C. Berkeley. He is a trial lawyer. He has studied classical guitar for decades. For fifteen years, he was a friend and poetry student of Jack Gilbert, until Jack's death. He was a 2019 National Poetry Series Finalist. His first book, *Naming the Wind*, was published by Omnidawn in 2022.